SPACE WALK

SPACE WALK

TOM SLEIGH

HOUGHTON MIFFLIN COMPANY *Boston   New York* 2007

For information about permission to reproduce selections from this book, write to Permissions, Houghton Mifflin Company, 215 Park Avenue South, New York, New York 10003.

Visit our Web site: www.houghtonmifflinbooks.com.

Library of Congress Cataloging-in-Publication Data
Sleigh, Tom.
  Space walk / Tom Sleigh.
    p. cm.
  ISBN-13: 978-0-618-68424-3
  ISBN-10: 0-618-68424-7
  I. Title.
  PS3569.L36S65 2007
  811'.54—dc22   2006030487

Book design by Melissa Lotfy

Printed in the United States of America

MP 10 9 8 7 6 5 4 3 2 1

The author would like to thank the following publications in which many of these poems were first published: *Agni:* "Invader," "Ziggurat." *Atlantic Monthly:* "Panel at the Press Club." *Colorado Review:* "Oracle." *Harvard Review:* "Necessity." *Hunger Mountain: Vermont College Journal of Arts and Letters:* "Chant," "Betrayal." *Kenyon Review:* "Achilles' Dream," "Blueprint," "Persian Miniature," "Song." *The New Yorker:* "Nobody." *Poetry:* "Fable," "Wall." *Poetry London:* "Archaic Figures." *Slate:* "The Hole." *Threepenny Review:* "The Breeze," "Space Station." *TriQuarterly:* "The Mouth." *Virginia Quarterly Review:* "Airport Economy Inn," "Last Broadcast." *Yale Review:* "Discipline," "Song Beyond Reason."

My deep thanks to Ellen, as always, and to Sarah and my friends.

CONTENTS

PART I

Blueprint

I had a blueprint
of history
in my head—

it was a history of the martyrs
of love, the fools
of tyrants, the tyrants
themselves weeping
at the fate of their own soldiers—

a sentimental blueprint,
lacking depth—
a ruled axis X and Y
whose illusions
were bearable . . .
then unbearable . . .

In that blueprint, I wanted to speak
in a language
utterly other, in words
that mimicked
how one of Homer's warriors
plunges through breastplate
a spear past
breastbone, the spearpoint searching
through the chest
like a ray of light searching
a darkened room
for the soul
unhoused, infantile,
raging—

but my figure of speech,
my "ray of light"—
it was really a spearpoint
piercing the lung
of great-hearted *Z*
who feels death loosen
his knees, the *menos*
in his *thumos*
flying out of him—

the fate of his own soul
to confront me
beyond the frame:

no room, no *X,* no *Y,* no "ray of light,"
no *menos,* no *thumos,* no *Z*—

only sketched-in plane
after plane after plane
cantilevering upward and forever throughout space.

Oracle

Because the burn's unstable, burning too hot
in the liquid-hydrogen suction line
and so causing vortices in the rocket fuel

flaming hotter and hotter as the "big boy"
blasts off, crawling painfully slowly
up the blank sky, then, when he blinks

exploding white hot against his wincing
retina, the fireball's corona searing
in his brain, he drives with wife and sons

the twisting road at dawn to help with the Saturday
test his division's working on: the crowd
of engineers surrounding a pit dug in snow

seeming talky, jokey men for 6 A.M., masking
their tension, hoping the booster rocket's
solid fuel will burn more evenly than the liquid

and keep the company from layoffs rumored
during recess, though pride in making
chemicals do just what they're calculated to

also keys them up as they lounge behind
pink caution tape sagging inertly
in the morning calm: in the back seat, I kick

my twin brother's shin, bored at 6:10 A.M.
until Dad turns to us and says, in a neutral tone,
Stop it, stop it now, and we stop and watch:

a plaque of heat, a roar like a diesel blasting
in your ear, heatwaves ricocheting off gray mist
melting backward into dawn, shockwaves rippling

to grip the car and shake us gently, flame
dimly seen like flame inside the brain confused
by a father who promises pancakes after,

who's visibly elated to see the blast shoot
arabesques of mud and grit fountaining up
from the snow-fringed hole mottling to black slag

fired to ruts and cracks like a parched streambed.
Deliriously sleepy, what were those flames doing
mixed up with blueberry pancakes, imaginings of honey

dripping and strawberry syrup or waffles,
maybe, corrugated like that earth, or a stack
of half-dollars drenched and sticky . . . ?

My father's gentle smile and nodding head—
gone ten years, and still I see him climbing
slick concrete steps as if emerging from our next-door

neighbor's bomb shelter, his long-chilled shade
feeling sunlight on backs of hands, warmth on cheeks,
the brightness making eyes blink and blink . . .

so like his expression when a friend came
to say goodbye to him shrunken inside
himself as into a miles-deep bunker . . .

and then he smiled, his white goatee
flexing, his parched lips cracked but welcoming
as he took that friend's hand and held it, held it

and pressed it to his cheek . . . The scales, weighing
one man's death and his son's grief against
a city's char and flare, blast-furnace heat melting

to slag whatever is there, then not there—
doesn't seesaw to a balance, but keeps shifting,
shifting . . . nor does it suffice to make simple

correspondences between bunkers and one man's
isolation inside his death, a death
he died at home and chose . . . at least insofar

as death allows anyone a choice, for what
can you say to someone who's father or mother
crossing the street at random, or running

for cover finds the air sucked out
of them in a vacuum of fire calibrated
in silence in a man's brain like my father's

—the numbers calculated inside the engineer's
imagination become a shadowy gesture as in Leonardo's
drawing of a mortar I once showed my father

and that we admired for its precision, shot raining
down over fortress walls in spray softly pattering,
hailing down shrapnel like the fountain of Trevi

perfectly uniform, lulling to the ear and eye
until it takes shape in the unforgiving
three-dimensional: as when the fragile,

antagonized, antagonistic human face
begins to slacken into death as in my own
father's face, a truly gentle man except

for his work which was conducted gently too—
since "technicals" like him were too shy for sales
or management, and what angers he may have had

seemed to be turned inward against judging
others so the noise inside his head was quieter
than most and made him, to those who knew him well,

not many, but by what they told me after he died,
the least judgmental person
they'd ever known—who, at his almost next to last

breath, uncomplaining, said to his son's
straining, over-eager solicitation,
—*Is there something you need, anything?*

—*That picture—straighten it* . . . his face smoothing
to a slate onto which light scribbles what? a dark joke,
an elegant equation, a garbled oracle?

Space Station

My mother and I and the dog were floating
Weightless in the kitchen. Silverware
Hovered above the table. Napkins drifted
Just below the ceiling. The dead who had been crushed
By gravity were free to move about the room,
To take their place at supper, lift a fork, knife, spoon—
A spoon, knife, fork that, outside this moment's weightlessness,
Would have been immovable as mountains.

My mother and I and the dog were orbiting
In the void that follows after happiness
Of an intimate gesture: her hand stroking the dog's head
And the dog looking up, expectant, into her eyes:
The beast gaze so direct and alienly concerned
To have its stare returned; the human gaze
That forgets, for a moment, that it sees
What it's seeing and simply, fervently, sees . . .

But only for a moment. Only for a moment were my mother
And the dog looking at each other not mother
Or dog but that look—I couldn't help but think,
If only I were a dog, or Mother was,
Then that intimate gesture, this happiness passing
Could last forever . . . such a hopeful, hopeless wish
I was wishing; I knew it and didn't know it
Just as my mother knew she was my mother

And didn't . . . and as for the dog, her large black pupils,
Fixed on my mother's faintly smiling face,
Seemed to contain a drop of the void
We were all suspended in; though only a dog
Who chews a ragged rawhide chew toy shaped
Into a bone, femur or cannonbone
Of the heavy body that we no longer labored
To lift against the miles-deep air pressing

Us to our chairs. The dog pricked her ears,
Sensing a dead one approaching. Crossing the kitchen,
My father was moving with the clumsy gestures
Of a man in a spacesuit—the strangeness of death
Moving among the living—though the world
Was floating with a lightness that made us
Feel we were phantoms: I don't know
If my mother saw him—he didn't look at her

When he too put his hand on the dog's head
And the dog turned its eyes from her stare to his . . .
And then the moment on its axis reversed,
The kitchen spun us the other way round
And pressed heavy hands down on our shoulders
So that my father sank into the carpet,
My mother rested her chin on her hand
And let her other hand slide off the dog's head,

Her knuckles bent in a kind of torment
Of moonscape erosion, ridging up into
Peaks giving way to seamed plains
With names like The Sea of Tranquility
—Though nothing but a metaphor for how
I saw her hand, her empty, still strong hand
Dangling all alone in the infinite space
Between the carpet and the neon-lit ceiling.

"Barbarian"

to a father-in-law

Tears that should have been wept over you weren't wept.
That's why, they said, during your dying, your eyes kept staring

Straight. *Barbarian,* was that what you thought
Of me, waiting for me to come, right before the end?

Did you envision scar tissue pricked out
In a perfect spiral all across my back?

I came to think of your eyes staring from
The eyeholes of what seemed like a helmet

The pain lowered over your face as eyes
Of bronze or of Parian marble, unmoving:

Fixing me where I stood, though I was far from you:
Fixing you all wrong: marble and bronze, for all

Their beauty, don't so much preserve as paralyze.
Your essence aches only in the gravures of the brain.

It's bad, knowing that your memory
Must outlive us: but your daughter and I

Suffer more than the sleeplessness and restless
Self-recriminations of a father's loss:

Barbarian: how hard it is to be free
When such a word afflicts you in the doubleness

Of passing as a Roman. For you, it was easy —
For you, the rites made the imperium

Assume you were one of them: Dear Father:
Your dying eyes stared straight — *stared straight* — in vain.

Barbarian: see: my face is painted blue
Like the savage Britons who denounce us

For making men slaves, for filling our granaries
With their harvests, for taking what we want

When we shelter in their houses, violating
Their wives and the sacred laws of hospitality.

And once I was one of them: I shouted into my shield
So that my battle cry rang loudest — but who among them

Would hear me now? And who among these Romans
Would know what my love of you has cost me?

Only you on your deathbed would be able to understand
What I would feel if I could see you lying there,

Too weak to move — you, my most feared,
Most trusted enemy . . . Now, for my absence,

For what my traitor heart felt and failed to do,
For what I yearned for in your kind eyes and frail embraces,

I know my every sigh must be held against me
Forever in that place you've gone to.

That place which even now I feel my soul
Knitting itself ever closer into yours.

—But for me it will be as with most men
Who have no name, no fame to call their own:

Some tears for me will be shed or not shed
Before *barbarian* is buried in oblivion.

The Breeze

for Ed Robbins

Like code for a lover's murmurings, MIA IED blew in
       on the breeze from some place other than the place
of pleasure I remember, bower too far ever

to get back to now in the alphabet war war was waging . . .
       The language of that breeze was fluent, calming,
its coolness almost chill but hoarding July heat

that would turn the dunes to an abstract shimmer
       jets from the base would penetrate, disappearing
an instant before piercing through glare, wings

tilting sunlight toward flattening ocean,
       a TV on somewhere down the leafy lane shrilling
a siren the breeze altered, catching it up, softening it

to almost human keening, though for what or whom
       the breeze wasn't saying: how disjunct it felt, the breeze
blowing some memory of distant pleasure mingling

with pleasure now of a body next to mine — my weirdness
       of thinking, as the breeze cooled my flank, of my friend
putting on his helmet and Kevlar vest, fitting the Kevlar

with a lover's gesture up between his legs so the family jewels
       would be locked away, and hearing him joking
this was the way the middle-aged of either sex ought always

to dress to go out to the bars, this was the way what
        the breeze wasn't saying and what my friend was
by not saying it, this was the way the acronyms

MIA IED partook of the breeze's other murky meanings—
        not saying what my friend would later show me,
all of it coming together so confusedly

but as if the breeze were words the acronyms
        spelled out before there were conditions to bring them
to the tongue rooting them in air, letter on letter

opening and flowering—oh come off it, fuck it, stop
        all this deployment of flowers and figures
to get around what was right there on the ground,

the glistering strangeness of it lying in the sun, skullcap
        blown off, thick black luxurious hair of a suicide
bomber, like a wig hung in a well-dressed window in one

of the salon-type places in an opulent mall, hair
        a breeze rippled ever so slightly, first this
hair, that, lifting, subsiding, the breeze stroking forelocks

and tresses that nestled on the shoulders minutes
        before my friend took the video—that breeze was blowing
across desert and ocean all the way to here, if only

in my mind thinking to join that soughing to this feeling
        of naked flanks cooling after waking a few inches
away, breeze flowing in the space between

cooling that place I wanted to get back to when the poem began
          but will never enter except in words the breeze does
or doesn't understand, Missing In Action, Improvised Explosive

Device taking on the aura of words the breeze spoke
          eons ago but before there was something like a war
to give them such repletion and ardor.

The Mouth

after a painting by Gerhardt Richter

The mouth was open and we stared into it—
what could we do about it, how could we stop staring?
The other people in the museum, weren't they staring too,
as if we were all under some spell we knew
couldn't be resisted, not that moment anyway
as we wandered inside the gallery
weirdly enchanted so that we couldn't look away:

the painting we were looking at was like a fire
waiting to be put out by the way we poured ourselves
into every detail of its making, its making so withheld
from us, saying *fuck you* to the viewer, *fuck you, stay away,*
like someone fearful of being struck or worse:
we were looking at a dead mouth that was the mouth
of Andreas Baader, Baader the scholar, Baader

the murderer of the Red Army Faction
being wound into the Sixties entwining him
into too bright, always constricting coils . . .
And then it was like the mouth swallowed us down
into unreflecting darkness and you and I slid
behind the palisade of teeth, the lump
of tongue like the dragon of Asgard

or like a monster in a movie about dying space creatures
who must couple with a human to survive:
deep inside that mouth, rising from the lungs
we could hear words breeding, unfathomable
or stupid, vulgar, foreign, words that rang
with the strangeness of *anangke* that Hercules
hears as the fate he must fulfill, slaughtering

with his club whatever comes into his way:
there was something foreordained but almost slapstick
about our sliding through that mouth's void
while the others kept on in their own separate ways of looking,
their plans for afterward made luminous
by the clarity of what we could see from that mouth
as we stared past the teeth and out the walls of glass

to the overgrown fens and transparency of sky
passing into sky, there was something out of bounds
about any kind of unhappiness or joy or fear
when we were here, in this mouth—which is what we were born for:
you and I who hadn't seen any of this coming,
you and I who also had plans after we left the museum,
there we were inside that mouth, eyes staring

in estrangement and alien wonder at the others.

Invader

"Seven furlongs of papyrus
and flax cables
lie shredded and entangled,
floating sodden

on the Hellespont's
storming waters,
the remains
of Xerxes' bridge,

Xerxes the Invader:
but you, Great King Xerxes,
chosen son of Cyrus,
you gave the waves

three hundred lashes,
you hurled chains
into those traitor waves,
you branded

their rebellious,
restless sides
with hissing irons.
Then you rounded up

the engineers,
chopped off
their heads:
then new engineers

took over, lashing
together triremes
and galleys,
360 vessels

moored head-on
to the current
to lessen the strain
on cables groaning;

then timbers
were laid down,
brushwood on timbers,
and finally earth

tamped over all,
basketful on basketful
trampled hard
by the cavalry's hooves;

and now, Great King Xerxes,
you sit on
your marble throne
high on the highest hill

above the plain of Abydos:
your troops swarm
the beaches and fill
every inch of ground,

your armada's sails
blot out the waves,
your centipeding oars
scuttle across

those subject waters:
for seven days and nights
day and night
the army crosses . . .

but look: the Great King weeps:
for he feels his fate
in all the arms and legs
milling beneath his eyes:

O what use to be a King,
what use to rule
East and West
from Susa

to Sparta's plains,
for in a hundred years' time,
not one of all my soldiers
will be left alive . . ."

after Herodotus

Necessity

I was trying, as always,
too hard.

My friend, who counseled
less intensity, hovered in the door,
smiling kindly—and then she was off
into her errands.

I looked at the room around me:
reproductions of a painting
of a mouth—

how badly
I wanted to put words
into that mouth—

to make that mouth
a hero's, to have it say
anangke, necessity—

and though the words
kept piling up, nothing
ever felt right, felt like it
measured up to my myth
of wanting life
to be not just a hero's life
but a hero-slave's
making constant
submission to his fate:

anangke—such a homely, recalcitrant sound;

what a god in his chariot drives straight
into the ear of my hero-slave bending down to hear,
as if to the mouths
of his wife and infant sons,
the word his ashen spear and never-failing sword
keep on whispering.

But of course I wasn't the hero-slave —
no god had raised me up
or raised a hand against me —

I could leave my room
any time I chose, the walls weren't mouths
chorusing
anangke:

I'd have to shape out of my habits
and limited self
a space
where that hero-slave could breathe —

as if my will to be that space
was oxygen in a tube —

a life support system
for the astronaut floating
in his clumsy suit
haplessly mimicking the gestures of earth,
gravity a reflex
he barely recalls,
the infinite void
more domestic than infinite,
life and death a matter
of checking his spacesuit's pressure gauge.

And then I looked out the window
into leaves—naked, massed, impenetrable,
still green—

though the more I stared, the more I saw
the first faint red tinge bleeding outward,
rooflines emerging
from where leaves were falling,
the air seemingly more clear than ever I had seen it—

the air that my Hector,
whom I love more than Achilles,
must breathe.

Ice Trucker Pilgrimage: A Libretto

I

The Universe Co., my infamous employer,
is devoted to keeping America cold—
and me, well, let's just say that the way God moves mountains,
I move ice.

Ice makes me kneel down for its benediction.
Ice cracks and fissures and splinters in my face.
I am destroyed by ice, by ice I am raised up.

The way Kafka believes in happiness as a condition
reserved for others,
the way God mainlines terror into an artery,
that's the way I believe in ice.

Look in my rearview mirror, and you'll see how cold pursues me:

it follows me wherever I go,
this zero at the bone,
this little iceberg I'm dragging down South toward the disaster,
what we Icemen call The Zone.

And if you listen real hard, underneath the engine roar
you'll hear an infernal humming:
a refrigerator unit embedded in my chest.

2

All across the city the glacier light keeps creeping.
Cold blue barbarian light,
northern light of Bruges,
the Master of the Blue Madonna light.

And lo, my eighteen-wheeler rig levitated above the earth.

I was watching a creature leap from ice floe to ice floe.

How long it had been out wandering the oceans of light.

Fear was walking its legs.
Anger was gesturing its hands.

The frozen sun stared down.

For miles and miles all across the city nothing else was moving.

3

The Zone is not for sissies, as Simone Weil would have said,
had she ever seen The Zone.

Broken gear teeth salting the earth.

Paranoid glitter of bridges collapsed in the rivers.

A black dog panting behind you, tongue red and steaming,
nose snuffling as if smelling soul-stuff
smoking underground.

The devastation is complete, not a house,
not a barricade,
not a tower left standing.

I enter into this place with all my senses on their knees.

This is the anti-pilgrimage, the Santiago de Compostela
of an Iceman.

The way an old pocketwatch ticks at night,
that's the way the flames leap inside the pilgrims' ears.

Ninety-one thousand tons of ice cubes won't quench that burning.

4

When the creature talks to God, God is like a tennis ball
he squeezes in his hand to make his wrist strong,
God exercises the creature's qualities of mercy.

All night the creature stays up staring into the TV screen,
studying it with the intimate urgency of a lover's face,
eyes searching for a sign of the city's coming annihilation.

God is so unpredictable to the creature.

And God grows a gourd that hangs in the creature's face,
and the creature rejoices,
then God sets a worm to shrivel the gourd.

And God chides the creature for his anger over the gourd,
but the creature holds to his anger like a life buoy,
he holds to it even unto death.

God sees how the creature weeps over the gourd.

God chastises the creature's grief and makes him sit
in frozen contemplation of the replay
of the house softly, slowly
sliding into the waves again and again,
the walls' languorous collapse caressing to the eye.

And the creature rises from sackcloth and ashes,
he rises against the wind to shelter the multitudes
who don't know their right hands from their left.

5

God pumps polar cold
back into the ocean so that the water knits itself
to slob ice hardening to a sheet so thick
nothing can dive deep enough
to swim underneath it:

the waters compass me about, the depths close round,
my rig's a submarine cruising night's black,
4,000 miles from Spartanville to Greenville, Carthage, Camp Shelby:

ice holds me fast in its burning grip.

6

The fans blew across the ice blocks.
Light rotated over the fan blades
and lit the faces of the dying.

The nurses in white coats wore the momentary chill
as if it was the ocean depths
breathing under the ice caps.

An embroidered picture of Frosty the Snowman
hung in a black frame
and the rest of the room seemed to kneel down before him.

An IV pole flashing silver above the darkened ward
was like the flag planted at the magnetic heart
of the South Pole.

I was headed there in my rig, but I was too late to save the creature
freezing in his tent, writing his last words in his diary:

For God's sake take care of our people.

Chant

Fountain of speech that would render us transparent gone
all muddy at the source. Nimbus of anger, that ballpeen hammer
pounding faintly in the temples. The Puerto Rican man,
in dapper wingtips and leather car coat, shouting:
I'm the customer, I paid my money, now get me my stuff,
his eyes boring in, *Oh the no good black man, and you,*
blanco, he waits on you before he waits on me.
The kid he shouts at, exploding: *Who you telling to get your stuff,*
I'm the worker, the worker, you're not my dumbass father.

Addled subjectivity fizzing over like a Pepsi in reruns
of a sitcom in which white father-in-law and black son-in-law
mouth scripted barbs, *All in the Family* vying to be funny, laughtrack
laughing at that Redneck, that Jungle Bunny, that Racist, that Fool.
Spanglish, Arabic, Yiddish, Urdu, Brooklynese, Haitian French.
Cruising full steam on minimum-wage labor, the forklift hefts pallets
for the men to unload: pyramids of paint cans, windows, doors,
prefab horn of plenty glutting the aisles. Motor's underdrone slurring
warning to the species but the frequency's too high or too low to be heard.

Gunite-sprayed posts and blackened beams hollowing out
a cavern under the city's towers. Omnium-gatherum on Jay Street
that calls itself Sid's Hardware: *If we don't have it, you don't need it.*
Helium feeling that makes you feel you're floating, dissolving to air
as their voices arguing reverberate down pilings pinging in the bedrock
two stories down while in other basements other voices ripple down
the girders like tuning forks set quavering, the city's granite schist singing
back to the shadowed mouths carved out of neon, voices tremulous
with laughter? anger? tears? some feeling too particular to be named?

Thesis, antithesis, synthesis in which all things human
and material are explained in words that don't slide off
and that everyone can understand though who controls such words,
who could say them? Refrigerator, osterizer, dehumidifier
piling higher and higher into a tower of Babel washed
by polyglot waters, speech rivers inundating the goods stacked up.
Atoms swarming into forms that stock the shelves
floor to ceiling as breath sighs over matter
like a wave playing over rock immovably eroding away.

Betrayal

My mother lying
>on her bed as on a raft
>>in a pond
was reading aloud
>for love
>>*Walden*'s ant war.

Words she read swelled the pond
>to an ocean
and I was swimming through
>sky that was
>>water
of her voice
>flowing with
>>an alien joy—

then she dove
>far beneath me
>>into the pages'
crystal depths
>while I floated on the surface
and peered down
>at her:
>>what her voice was describing

was terrible:
>two red ants
>>severing
the feeler
>of a giant
>>black ant twice their size

and the mandibles of that giant
                              ripping
through the breastplates
                              of the red ants gnawing
in fatal embrace
                    "and so
                              there were three
united for life
                    as if a new kind
of attraction
                    had been invented
that put all other locks and cements
                                        to shame."

Her voice reading
                    sounded like pleasure,
a current
          of cold water streaming
                              into hot—
the two swept up
                    into the ocean stream
that carried her so far
                    beyond the bedroom
I was waving to her
                    to come back in to shore—
not leave me for those
                    words
                              rising up
over my head,
                    me swimming like an ant
caught in the current
                    as I watched
                              her joy so inward

and obscure,
                    treacherous joy
                              I'd learn from
her mouth . . .
                    and so learn to build
                                        my own raft
drifting farther and farther past
                              the pillars
of the world
                    her voice piled up around me
stone on stone
                    until those pillars
                              I sailed past
shrank into the sun
                    crawling down the blank
blue wall
          of sky
                    in the prime of my clear
and strong-voiced mother
                              reading out the words
to her co-conspirator
                    whose desire,
as he listened,
                    was to be lured down into
the sensual muck
                    of her shipwrecked mind
and breathe in her words
                              like bubbles of air
that one day would turn me
                              into her traitor's
traitor:
          never again would she
                              abandon

me
      on shore
             because of my own
voyaging
             in abandonment of
                          her
in our words'
             mutual, estranging
                          pleasure.

The Hole

Out in the garden, the wind was like a dog
digging in the snow, digging with its nails
to make a bed to lie down in against the freezing air:

and in my exhaustion, my stupefied numb thought
dug and dug its way down to where I knew
you were—though how could I believe it?

Once, your irony and honesty refused
to let you say, "Oh yes, my son the genius!"
when I showed you a poem—saying with Groucho deadpan,

as you handed me back the paper, the typed words
already a little smudged: "Hopkins is a good poet."
And then you recited, *"Margaret, are you grieving*

Over Goldengrove unleaving? . . ." winking
at the poets not yet born . . . poets who would
come after me, poets who would not believe

there was any such woman as you,
who would say of them and their poetry,
shrugging a little, smiling your sly, lopsided grin:

"How old are you, hon? From what I've read,
your sex life must be very important to you."
Digging in the snow, digging with its nails

down deep in the snow, the wind kept trying
to hollow a hole deep enough to escape its own bitter
blowing of snow around the frozen garden.

Nobody

Line after line smearing off into elephantine
scrawls as she tries to recall which way
the pencil goes, my friend's wife who can't organize
her mind to spell out her name sits staring

at the bookshelf bowed under the weight
of the thousand thousand rivulets of print
she can't remember writing. Her mind keeps scabbing
over—and then she picks it and picks it

until it bleeds . . . and she's herself again,
her heart rejoicing that she's Anne and not
someone other who afflicts her like a stranger

hiding in her bedroom, whispering with affable,
red-faced jocularity that if you're nobody
and nobody's tormenting you why do you cry out?

Drag Show

The Nineties, Eighties, Seventies peel away—
an unread obit eats up the entire day,
a single body warms the sheet's chill.

What sex is, what we want it to be—
feeling myself haunted by the ghost of another,
I get dressed up to get undressed with a stranger,

AIDS and STDs in the background
like noise from the radio turned down . . .
How many wager on taking off their clothes

but never putting them back on?
At the midnight drag show we sing along
with Cher, boobs heaving as she belts out

"Half Breed," the allegory of being split
lending glamor to the outlaw outcast
who now comes back as the avenging angel,

Joan Rivers in lamé haranguing
over and over her carnal duet
raunchy with tenderness and smut:

And remember this, Ladies, that overcharging
chiseler of an undertaker gets
to cop a last feel, he oughtta pay us!

The crowds jostle on Commercial Street,
the meat-rack benches packed with living meat
like an affront to all those spirit-bodies

still hungry to sniff and quaff the blood—
they grope like streetlight through sliding mist,
penetrating our bodies the way x-rays

beaming from the Coast Guard radar
map the cloud-up out beyond the waves.
Slipping in and out of us, making it together,

dead Jims, Mikes, Celias, Sues congregate in wet flickers
wavering down a wine glass, in the many-eyed spangle
of a belt buckle unclasped and falling to the floor.

You, who come back to me every night,
I feel you travel at the speed of light away
from bars and cafés and people making out . . .

If only your face would flare
before going dark in lighthouse light
strobing across the dunes vaporous and separate . . .

Footsteps move stairs to bathroom, bathroom to bed.
The cellphone glows a moment on my pillow,
the ringer, set to vibrate, waiting for your call:

—If you need anything, just whistle.
You know how to whistle, don't you?
You just put your lips together and blow.

Tonight

After rain
plastered cherry blossoms
to the sidewalk we
were freer than we knew—
twenty years
in each other's weather
and we could almost laugh
at our rain-spoiled futures—

love cut us one way,
then split along the grain.

But tonight I wanted to read you
Donne's last days:
winding sheet knotted
at hands and feet,
he stands
on his urn, eyes shut, sheet
pulled aside
to show his lean
pale face
turned to the East
where he expects the body,
the blood
of his risen lover
who comes closer the closer he comes
to being lost;
but it's only the moon's
nailholes glinting
in midnight sun,

dead aura sweating on his brow.
Donne, who knows
he's dying, keeps posing
for the painter
who draws him lifesize
on a board
so that in his sickness
he can contemplate
his dying likeness.

How much shall I be changed
before I am changed—

but tonight, for us,
no promise of heaven, no threat of hell—
just this sickroom quiet of my old fever
we feared so often
our years together . . . my faithful infirmity
the one ritual I keep, your absent hand
warm on mine.

Through the lamp's half-dark
I stumble to the bathroom,
kneel down before the bowl
and rest my head against the toilet paper roll,
its soft three-ply
sweet-scented, tender,
like saying a prayer
I want to believe in—
a prayer
I pray to, not for
you—the words
not words
but articulate whines

pleading like a dog
to be let in after having been let out
only a moment before—
my face less human
than a dog's
as I kneel on all fours,
tail wagging
to smell you again,
hoping to be fed
before lying down
under the unrumpled,
too strictly made bed.

How can I talk to you in the old mongrel way,
two as one, the one coming undone
to less than either?

After Nietzsche

for Ellen

Not merely bear what is necessary,
still less conceal it—
all idealism is mendaciousness
in the face of what is necessary—
but love it.

Love it, not merely bear it
in the face that must conceal it:
mendaciousness of idealism
not able to bear what is necessary—
not merely bear it but love it.

In the face that must conceal
what is necessary
to bear
love appears in the face
of the face of what is necessary.

PART II

Last Broadcast

"We, the most far away people

                on the earth,

the last of the free

                shielded until today

by our remoteness

                and obscurity,

even here we know

                what everybody knows:

that those who know

                little about us

are by their very ignorance

                convinced we are a prize:

beyond us there's nothing

                but rocks and waves

and our invaders

                more deadly than these—

bowing in submission,

                escaping in a boat

won't keep them in their arrogance

                from killing us.

Pillagers of the world

                a rich enemy excites

their cupidity, a poor one

                their avarice for power.

East and West they

                devour, and still they must

have more.

                Rich or poor, their greed

drives them to rapine,

                robbery, butchery—

and this

        they call 'government.'

Everywhere they are

        is wiped out

in desolation — and this

        they call 'peace.' "

after Tacitus

Premonition

Oh yes, banality of mind to think
itself safe just because out there you
can see the first faint green of unkillable

weeds spring up in the sidings,
thistles that by summer will shake
and sway in breeze the trains

set swirling . . . oh yes, this fool's
paradise my mind lives in, thinking
to make itself secure: moving through

the days, rounding each corner,
nerve-endings like radar scan
the ether for this new tremor

passing in a dream through the body
of a soldier or through my wife's hand
lifting to drink a glass of water,

unnoticed in the day-to-day crisis chatter—
an animal alertness sensing in the air
some predator closing, the soft footpads

setting off minute vibrations so infinitely
penetrant they cleave earth's core
so that trees coming into leaf quake with it

so subtly nobody can see, only sense
that quaking until you feel it
upsetting some balance tipping

tipping, gone suddenly too far, tumbling
over and over, arms reaching
out to grab grabbing only air.

Panel at the Press Club

She who had most trouble saying anything
at all, expressionless in her blue blazer
and white silk shirt and sipping her glass of water
and looking away, eyes far from everything,

she who knew firsthand, what was it she was thinking? —
the others' earnest voices rang out eerily
somnambulant, equivocating over "enemy,"
tongues to a high gloss polishing

"freedom" "casualty" "most regrettably"
"that's where the force comes in" — but what was it
she was thinking — remembering, maybe,
how during the bombardment she sat

hunched in her apartment, watching water
tremble, slosh, ripple, smooth over
until the next shockwave through I-beams
rises, fish darting into her aquarium's

corners, ornamental blue crests wavering,
striped gills fluttering, fins twitching
to explosions rolling through what
she called, betraying no emotion, "rocket streets"?

Persian Miniature

Purple-backed, clambering
through prongs of grass
a beetle moves at eye-level
where stripped
to his underwear, hands bound behind back,
rocks digging into knees, he kneels
in the ditch, cheek resting against damp clay
as if rain fell when bombs fell a day or two before.
Beard still freshly trimmed, he must have fallen
into enemy hands just this morning,
the perspective down the ditch receding prisoner
to prisoner shrinking smaller, smaller,
until all you can see is the faintest blur
of skin and hair.
Neck and shoulders taut from
the strain, musculature ridged up on either side
of his spine, the popping
vertebrae lead to his ear's dark-shadowed hole:
when will the interrogations begin,
what spirit or demon
will slip inside his thoughts
nestled in his fragile skull?

Which turns one's thoughts
to his captors, the presumed victors —
a young man, wearing thick
prescription lenses that make him look even
younger and harder to read, stands one foot
on the ground, the other lifted in mid-air
as if he climbed an invisible ladder rising

from an island of duffel bags and packs—
holding his A3-GS
switched to automatic fire, behind him
the mosaic dome rising to a thin gold spire,
in his oversized boots and desert camouflage
he seems dwarfed by his uniform,
a diminutive figure
balanced mid-rung that climbs
from stones of the ditch past a white flower
prickling and itching the prisoner's chest,
ascending past
animals like jackals that can't be far off,
to the many rents
in his own fabric of man
and so on up to spirits
corporeal and incorporeal to God whose bound
is nowhere and circumference everywhere:

the nowhere-everywhere of God the Leader
shadowed forth in the dictator's
statue stiff on its plinth, marble hand held out
to bless, while behind him flames
fur the air as if the fire were mange
itching at the statue raised above
the burning city
balanced on its ladder-rung of the invisible
reaching upward to graze the stars
in this "man-masse" of antipathies:
"private and domesticke enemies within,
publicke and more hostile adversaries without . . .
So let me be nothing if within the compasse
of my selfe I doe not find the battel
of Lepanto, passion against reason,
reason against faith, faith against the Devill,

and my conscience against all.
There is another man within me that's angry
with me, rebukes, commands and dastards me."
A scraggly date palm ghosts upward
through greasy smoke
while fire shinnies up buildings
as it scurries roof
to roof, clearly limning
two towers' crenelations,
orange flames darkening to purple
burning whatever's there until it's not,
that ladder burning downward to the ground.

Zoom

In that flickering smoky light if you haven't got a rocket

would a stone stand for a rocket in the hand hurling it? —

the stone hurled to consummation,

the uniformed body lifted to the women's ululation

while we, the invisible watchers, join in silent chorus

above the mere meat now dragged in front of us,

the helmet sliding off, torso limp, eyes unmoving

reflected reversed in glass blankly shining,

the panes blowing out in soft slow motion

toward the camera lens that sees unshaken

aere perennius fire sheets raining down

bringing us up close expanding with the zoom.

Ziggurat

What's built collapses
to be rebuilt, ruin on top
of ruin piling up into
a ziggurat pocked by shell holes

so that our knowledge is the knowledge
of drifting sand, grit in the cupboard,
grit under the bed where a doll's head,
button eyes open, lies forgotten.

We will be covered by the dune
and uncovered in time,
our helmet straps wasted away,
metal eaten through—

though we, the fallen, perpetually
on guard, will stare back at you
from the streaked bathroom mirror,
making yourselves presentable to the light of day.

For us, the marshlands drained and turned
to dust will be our present kingdom,
our spectral waterway among the always instant reeds,
shivering, bending to the current.

Fable

A LITTLE VILLAGE IN TEXAS HAS LOST ITS IDIOT
read the caption on a protest sign —

but where, oh where is the holy idiot,
truth teller and soothsayer, familiar

of spirits, rat eater, unhouseled wanderer
whose garble and babble fill rich and poor,

homeless and housed, with awe and fear?
Is he hiding in the pit of the walkie-talkie,

its grid of holes insatiably hungry,
almost like a baby, sucking in the police sergeant's

quiet voice as he calls in reinforcements?
Oh holy idiot, is that you sniffing the wind

for the warm turd smell on the mounted policemen
backing their horses' quivering, skittish

haunches into the demonstrators' faces?
Oh little village among the villages,

the wild man, the holy Bedlamite is gone,
and nobody, now, knows where to find him . . .

Lying in mud? lying caked in mud, hair elfed into knots?
Some poor mad Tom roving the heath

for a warm soft place to lay his body down,
his speech obsessed with oaths, demons,

his tongue calling forth the Foul Fiend, Flibbertigibbet
as the horses back slowly, slowly into the crowd

and he eats filth, he crams his ravenous mouth with filth —
and then he sits on his stool in the trampled hay

and deep-rutted mud, he anoints himself
with ashes and clay, he puts on his crown

of fumiter weed and holds his scepter
of a smouldering poker and calls the court to order.

Wall

On this side of the wall, the well-lit room
lights gilt pages that luxuriate

in ornate capitals commemorating kings,
while there, on the other side, smoke and fire

press against the wall, where the stick-figure soldier
huddles away from the explosions, dwarfed

by the smoke column rising. The young Marine
at Quantico who calls me on his cell

feels the full weight of the wall pushing up
beyond the barracks walls he lives in,

swaying in the sun, swaying as if to
fall on him as he focuses on Clausewitz,

Sun Tzu's *Art of War,* Commandant Gray's *Warfighting* . . .
The wall ripples from the ground on up into

the sun, and only if you let go of your
human shape and only if your body

bleeds into the wall's flat vertical
can you feel that altitude and lift

as in an elevator shooting to
the top so that even when it stops

you feel yourself hurtle through the air:
hold on to yourself if you enter the wall's

sub-atomic storm, where everything is motion
and not the huge kings or tiny foemen

snarled in gilt vines can keep safe from the wounds
seeping through the wall to where the soldier

smoothes back his hair, the bombardment healing over
to the puckered, ashen smoulder of a scar.

PART III

Song Beyond Reason

The air's blank September heat
                              breathes into my window,
summer revives
                    in the massed green heads
of the waiting trees, waiting to write in leaves
their technicolor epitaphs,
                              brittle, wheezy sayings
rattling in the breeze.
                        All summer's the season
when love,
          beyond reason, flourished
and failed, failed and refined itself
                              to golden
Scotch floating two rocks melting in the glass.
No matter how close love comes,
                        no matter
how we move away from love
                        to understand
the terms September imposes and demands,
the heavens don't sanction
                        our onanistic spacewalks
out among the genitalia of the stars.
Summer gave our hands to others
                        so that giving
became a wound you studied
                        as its scholar—
and then the scar takes love's place.
                        Summer fantasy
rules night and day—and it isn't empty—
though absurd to think the trees
                              have shadowy thoughts,

the un-ironic trees

         meditating happiness, unhappiness,
the jeweled, insectile

          loves, hates, the tyrant needs . . .
All summer was the season someone looked
at you, wanted you, and you felt the too giddy
fullness

     of a balloon rising in the air,
swelling to a knowledge of remorseless paradise,
not knowing it must burst,

         fall back to earth

a rag.

    All summer was the season
beyond dread or reason

         of happiness others
speak of sometimes, though maybe a little ironically,
not wanting to jinx it by naming it,
not wanting the prospect of air

        thinning into
air to dry up

    like spit or sperm or sweat.

Afterlife

The crowd's young in the café,
time wasting away to the ticking
of six clocks from different time zones.

The bathroom looms up
full of fortune cookie portent,
some guy in the next stall stinking up the place—

Time doesn't reveal us it unmasks us.
I'm staring at the wall and the wall's staring back:
smell of sulfur, sweat, beer,

the guy's body is making noises so strange
in the afterglow of talking over with you
the reasons why you want to leave—

my head feels disconnected
from what's going on down below
and I'm reveling in the guy's stink

as if it told me a kind of truth about myself:
I can't think of how to put it into words—
like the feeling you get when sun

lies down on water and a ladder of glare
follows you everywhere
inviting you into the sun's fire

where you'd burn up in a second:
something like that, and something
like a swallow smashing into a window

that keeps on beating its wings
as if it willed tomorrow looming up like glass:
I finish, wash my hands: the toilet flushes

with a satisfying suck. Pain's never
so articulate as when it can't find the words
but stains the heart the variegated colors

of shit we take for granted. That old fucker
Lear, he knew what he was doing,
going through the motions of his grieving,

his dead daughter in his arms
while a rat a dog a cat had life and she
no breath at all. The guy comes out of the stall,

and he's so handsome, so perfect in his white shirt,
his jeans, the hair on his well-muscled arms
light and downy. He leaves me standing there,

pretending to comb my hair but really
just looking at my face in the water-stained mirror
reflecting the wall green and black and brown.

Back in the café, at the table next to ours,
they're playing chess, taking their sweet leisure
as queens and pawns fall, the kings

seeming unconcerned moving one square
at a time before being maneuvered
up to the edge of their flat-earth kingdoms.

You're still there, and the talk starts again,
the vodka blinking back the sun, and the stink
off the sea makes me oddly happy.

Clinic

The name the nurse calls ripples down the corridor:
unspoken privacies speak in the women's eyes
as their anxious hands, lifting to their hair, freeze

as if caught in a convex mirror by an unseen painter
who, if he chooses, can paint into being cheeks of fat,
heart, lungs, spinal cord that sparks the birth-cry

still wawling in the younger women's futures;
while for others the lucent ovum won't darken
again with sperm . . . Queenly bulk still hidden,

these bellies won't stretch into globes
whose latitudes will be lavish
as the ermine-trimmed velvet robe

of the young, pale bride, her husband's face gravely
tender, his hand on her hand on her bulging belly
shadowed by death from septicemia.

In the young women's ears "the procedure" whispers
protocols—and in one older one's, her cheekbones
round and high as the painted girl-wife who will die;

the younger ones look up at her, her crowsfeet
attractive in a face so kind
that the others' sidelong stares look startled . . .

Outside, no picketers carry signs
neatly scrawled in red crayon by their own children:
SUFFER THE LITTLE CHILDREN TO COME UNTO ME!!!

Dust spirals into a double helix interlacing
across sunglare in the waiting room mirror
as the blinds rule out the cool March light in a gridiron

that crosses the older one's face and hands:
the clinic door beckons, the nurse again calls her name,
she wades through the television's low-voiced drone.

The room pitching and rolling in waves of neon
is like a ship on the horizon sailing into the sun
as into the too bright dream of the merchant husband,

his child-wife's face and his baby's face come streaming
across the reef ripping the hull, splintering, grinding—
all this is written in the papers of the young merchant

grown old along with his second wife
and their two daughters married in 1456 and 1459
"to sons with not insufficient dowries" . . .

And now, it's your turn—you walk through the clinic door,
your beauty's not untouchable, you are a woman in a woman's body
in your jeans and gray sweatshirt and pink sneakers,

you move down the hall to the examining room, you put
on your gown, the anaesthetic numbs but not enough
not to feel the vacuum hurt as walls fall away and you're out

walking among vegetable stalls, the blinding canals floating
red madder dyes, a persimmon brought back from countries
of the sun, a leek, a lopped turnip top flashing bright green.

Lullaby

My boy, my child,
what have I done?

It's true, by making you,
I sealed the order
for you to die—
forgive me, but when you fuck,
you make bodies who grow up
and make babies
of their own—

this is a fact
and doesn't
need to be atoned—
you know how a father's
light industry
of fears holds you hostage:

little arrow of ego
who flies into the future,
it's your face brimming
at the target's center.

But why pretend
a father's concern?
Why fuck with the head
of a kid
never born—

and why ask these dumb questions
when it's only on paper
that I hold you in my arms,
rhyming "born"
with "mourn,"
keeping you safe from harm,
safe from me,
my own, my child,
safe from this poem
you'll never see.

To a Wasp on Fifth Avenue

on the eleventh anniversary of my father's death

Your faceted eyes in their huge sockets swivel
like an antique pocketwatch's balance wheel,
the street in your stare multiplying to endless
avenues of air that you in your lightness

get blown down, each instant an eon
as you live out your afternoon
inspecting the corner deli's acid-rain
eaten sill, oh to light there beside you in

February's mumbling dementia . . . In an hour
you'll stiffen, mist locking you in ice until your
brash buzz freezes to comet-light, the poison
in your stinger held in solution

for the future as you scout the windowpane,
your hot plush jacket making the air numb
with false spring, as if your flight out of season
injected in my vein this dizzying sensation

of space kneeling down to cup us in its palm—
can this be you? Will you dare to land,
your antennae gently tapping my black-gloved hand,
my head a ghost nest ready to loose its swarm,

your stinger quivering just above my wrist
in a display of what? fear, joy, our old double-edged trust?
Father wasp, love still potent with pain,
in my buzz and burr will you know me as your own?

Hammer

Redwings cling to cattails
while a hammer hammering nails
rings an octave higher
at each *thwack thwack,* the overtones
decaying deliciously slowly.

And in that decay
day presses down on nothing,
though the tide spews up old tires gleaming,
suppository treasures, plastic smoothed
to an abalone shine.

I'm useless as a hammer found
floating in the brine, seeming weightless
on the sand as if it were that hammer
left floating on the moon
by a long-dead astronaut:

its lunar existence
absently posthumous,
it hovers in the ice age night
and crematory day.
Its weightlessness would make it nauseous

if it weren't dumb steel expanding, contracting—
forever subject to laws it cannot know
it doesn't feel,
it exists in a desert so absolute
no molecule of rust can taint its shining.

I see your hand reach out to it
but it keeps floating away:
the steel shank and phallic head
drift in the cushioning void,
dreaming of a nail

penetrating a lover's flesh.
The only other thing moving
over the moon's pitted face
is a long-forgotten flag
feeding its stripes into the void.

When the moon finally wakes
and breaks earth's orbit
it will be younger than the earth,
it will take up the hammer
and kiss it on the mouth.

Song

The lace under your shirt,
intricate as lichen,
flirts all night
with the moon's

distant interweaving that nobody
can hold
because it falls equally
on all this spring so cold

and late arriving—
twenty-five years to discover
that love still lies waiting . . .
Our talk builds in the air

nothing noble or simple
but something unforeseen
in the way people
come to mean

more than any presence
in the sky's vast foyer
leading to apartments
too grand for

easy habitation:
I love the way your face
becomes the reflection
of gravity, grace, a place

to settle in when
love that passes on
to others as soon as we are gone
arrives without an invitation:

let's lay our heads down
among beams and girders
rising floor by floor
around the moon half risen.

The Flood

Wave on wave on wave drowns the bedroom.
Waterlights play across our faces.
The fathoms above us unwaveringly clear, almost to radiance,

while below us, the sea keeps shelving down and down
to a bottomless blackness out of which a voice
speaks in compassionate, level tones:

"The clinical fear of breakdown is itself
a breakdown which has already taken place
—primitive agony—and there are moments

when the patient needs to be told that this
breakdown which he fears and is already
wrecking his life, has already occurred."

Think of what that voice must see and hear
in the deep to speak so clearly and calmly
of breakdown, things like breakdown.

Now, the old W. C. Fields line about why Fields
prefers whiskey to water resounds with the force
of scriptural law: *Because fish fornicate in water.*

And the corollaries too, fish shit and sleep
and eat and wake and swim and die in water,
the water a maw of fish stink and death

only intensifies the beauty of the water,
this watery clairvoyance we stare up into:
is this a vision of happiness then?

Ocean holding itself unto itself?
Water clear almost to invisibility?
Are these the conditions that we share,

the sea filtering us as if we were air
flowing in and out of each other's lungs?
We stare up at the bottom of a boat

floating in a slick of sun that casts
a shadow rocking back and forth, side to side,
never stopping, as if the water were

a kind of itching burning itself into
that shadow and the shadow scratched and
scratched and scratched the itch of the clear water.

Inventory

Her mouth. Her hand. Her way of speaking.
What daily she is and gives without knowing.

Her smallest gesture writing the rare
Compactness of her feeling on the air.

Knowledge of the code or syllabary,
Hieroglyphic sign, of her generosity.

How often lost to my lack, hesitation, fear
. . . I who sought and still seek to find her

And hope to seek no matter how or where
Until failing health or mind or whatsoever

Comes between us in final severance
Of mouth and hand, undoing our endurance.

Rune of her face intricate to decipher
With the lazy tracing of one finger.

Her gravity, transparency, her distance.
Our difference as we keep coming into balance.

Her voice inside of mine, mine inside of hers.
What I ask that her silence coolly answers.

Her turning away. Her turning toward.
Shifting of her focus turning inward.

Ghost-life of all the phantoms that we are
Coming between us as we move closer.

The long continuance that leads us where
The other comes constantly so near.

Broken Ballad

Moving closer to what love is
leaves me stranded on my single bed
in the redshift zone of my desire.
So much fantasy short-circuiting what moves

the planets and the stars, though never
could I exist out there without my moonsuit
impervious to stony meteorite,
though that's what I craved and plotted for

before craving became its own atmosphere.
Then love acknowledged there was no leader
to take me to — only this awkwardness
of fumbling hands, evasive eyes

that sometimes were mine, sometimes another's.
At such peaks of human exposure
I felt my face-plate slipping loose
and the inner face, an intricate map

of pits and craters, reveal to my lover
just why and where and how my dream
of love would push out death
the way space abhors a vacuum.

But even in that, I feared love's leaving —
every earthly thing spun free
from the subtle grip of gravity . . .
Bearing with the years, I found my love

in the underground like the one in the movie
about the apes that hate humankind,
rusty rails undergirding the ruined city
running parallel away from laws of steel

I trailed in hope and wary exhaustion
to this infinite place of wanting that wanted me:
as if wheels hauled me to the edge
of space walled up, gleaming, paranoid,

but vulnerable too, the stars like a ledge
I stepped out on and felt the semblance of home:
table, bed, chair; a door closing in my head
on that infinitely expanding room.

Block and Bag

Pursuit, delay, anxious moments of dallying,
then leaps, bounds, hilarious cartwheels turning
manic with rage or fear performed in a concrete

courtyard bare but for hotel windows replicating
everywhere these mad, senseless, random chases,
a little styrofoam block fiery as Achilles

racing after a plastic bag kiting and billowing
round and round this blah arena, this angle/plane world
stripped to extremes of sun scraping concrete

bare, or blasted dark, obliviated by clouds,
the light neutered to the spirit's dullest grays while Block
and Bag now seem hunter/prey, john/whore,

then inexplicably bound and flutter to a halt,
exhausted, Block's corners pitted, rounded
by bumps and skids and somersaults,

Bag blowzy and worn, bedraggled by all this
unexpected passion, this afflatus of breath swelling
it full then sucked out so it collapses in ruin,

abject, pleading, overdoing it maybe, knowing more
than it lets on, only playing dead for Block's titillation,
You did it, you conquered, I'm nothing, nothing . . .

until the whirlwind hits and drives them on
obsessed without purpose in their abandon
that could be joy, terror, elation of love, despair's

deflation, desire's movements like armies
maneuvering across no man's land, the spirit
coquetting after the unreachable

as Block now bounds to within an inch of Bag
fluttering off at an eccentric angle,
the light winking off it like an eye winking,

you know I know you know someone's watching—
now Bag crumples in a corner, seemingly blacked out,
Block hovering near as if debating to strike

and demolish Bag, put an end to this pursuit—
no angle of approach, no middle ground,
no terms of ransom, no truce—

just this squarish, brick-faced concrete
among endless displacements rippling out
across this nowhere courtyard where Block and Bag

are at it again, running amok, racing round and round,
giving no quarter and desiring none
the way heroes of old lavish on each other

ferocious attentions no lover can rival,
oh most worthy and wedded of combatants:
berserk Block; shrewd tactician Bag.

Archaic Figures

Ali's fists come flying from the past
with left jab, man-killing combination
snapping back the head
braving a concussion,
sweat mixing with blood trickling through salve
down the forehead of Chuck Wepner, 1975,
archaic now as Stallone or Schliemann.

—Three rapes this past week in my neighborhood,
Boerum Hill, Gowanus Houses:
the young woman cop said,
"If I find him, I tell you—
this hand will be the last he ever holds."

On a poetry gig, I went to a prison
and there I met a rapist who loved Ali,
who loved Apollo Creed and Rocky.
He worked out on the heavy bag each day
and sometimes he was Rocky smashing Apollo,
but more often he was Apollo smashing Rocky.

And some days he thought things were OK
and every time he hit the bag
the heart in his chest,
whirling like a lion at dogs
snapping at his haunches
or flying whining from his punishing paw,
would rejoice and laugh,
and some days he thought the world
was like a boulder hurled at him, dust
whirling round it

thundering downhill
choking the air as he ran one step
in front of that rock looming larger
and larger over his shoulder —
a rapist doing time . . .
You got to pay back society what you owe —.

Back in 1975, a woman told a class
what it was like —
said she stared into the gun
and it was like the barrel
was a tunnel
she had to walk down
into a cave so dark
you start to feel it's not you there at all,
and all you can hear is your own heartbeat.
— She didn't cry, or do any of the things
she'd have done on a show like *Law and Order;*
she simply told the story and was silent.

Silent as Apollo and Rocky
before the cameras
start rolling, the music pumping
while the heavy bag hangs
all night in the dark gym
and the tallest brick tower of the Gowanus Houses
shines in perfect delineation in the full moon.

A fist comes flying with grace and swiftness
like nothing other than an archaic figure
sung by the blindman Homer,
a fist both like and unlike
the fist at the end of the arm of the rapist
whose name, also, is Homer.

First Love

Leaves crunching as that other walked away,
the gun barrel like a tunnel he forced her to walk down,
she tells it now to the radio's static, lying in my arms
our very first date, her eyes shut tight,
her being contracted to a single point of pain
until she heard next to her ear an acorn's
pock and opened her eyes on its tough, pitted crown.

This pillow talk she tells you, confidant, lover for the night,
as you wonder what it's like for her, having you,
wanting you near, her trust so intimately
estranging as she tells you what he did to her
that even as you hold her you want to pull away:
and what makes her want to tell you, fear, disgust,
anger at what men might be, and some men are?

Acned, scared, your mattress huge, then too small,
and there she lies having told you all—the heater coil glows
too close to your face while inside your head the image of her lying
out there in the leaves haunts the body lying in your bed . . .
Afterward, you watch her sleep—and wonder what she knows
that you can't know about what love means,
means inside the body your bodies together make,

so vulnerable in its contours and shame, old shame
that is knowledge you must claim, your secrecy
of heart binding you together by
driving you apart even as you lie there
hoping she's enjoyed it, hoping her eyes
when she wakes won't flinch away and that your eyes
won't betray what you've been thinking.

Discipline

Random meeting at a bar,
          random association that didn't
need to happen, was it me
          feeling and saying what I said,
shaky after, but at the moment
loosening to friendship
          during time of war?—

he had good biceps,
          straight teeth, fancy sneakers.
Then he showed a pic of
          his soldier lover: tall, skinny,
appealing in a young Abe Lincoln way:
"When's he come home?"
          "Six months but he

already got extended ninety days."
He looked so young—and what? was it
          heat building in my gaze as we
stared together, desire crossing
          boundaries so that me thinking
I'm straight, my war Vietnam
began to chafe at strict

                    division enforced along lines
of discipline laid down
of what naked bodies do
                    and uniformed bodies don't? —
anyway, shouldn't a patriot want
                    to go to bed to solace a soldier
as handsome as this one, to feel pressure

of his eyes hard against
                    mine, his body in the line
of fire conspiring to let me move
                    closer, closer . . .
then the lover took out a letter from his soldier
                    that he showed me in a what? subtle gesture
of flirtation I just as subtly invited,

aware even in my straightness
                    I was over the line, voyeur
to myself, the war, the lover and his soldier
                    writing home how hot
                    the sun got, he'd shot a rubber bullet
into a crowd, he was going a little nuts
like those movies where the soldier always loses it —

the crowd was yelling, running, crossing
                    a line, zigging,
zagging, someone
                    stumbled, went down —
I turned my gaze from the photo's
smiling eyes, heat building in my looking
                    burning off and leaving

us awkward, cooling in
the once companionable dark:
                              "You must miss him."
"Well, you can see how

                    tall he is. His feet hung over
the edge of the bed. He

                    makes an easy target."

And then we get up to go,

                    me to come here, losing, then finding another
like him and his soldier

                    and the war far away
in these words but still

                    going on, each walking his own
shifty line of discipline.

Achilles' Dream

adapted from The Iliad, *Book XXIII*

The soldiers ate, drank; and then, exhausted, their food
making them yawn, they crowded into their tents,
they slept;
                but the son of Peleus,
no, the son of Peleus didn't sleep:
                              if you'd been there
with a camera, if you'd taken his picture,
a cruddy snapshot snapped in bad light,
the flash giving his face the look of someone at a party
who holds a candle just under his chin,
that's what you'd have seen:
                          eyes red,
face drained white; a shape blurry and huge
as an All Pro defensive end, a Big Daddy Lipscomb
crying out his eyes in desolation.

                            The long, flat, clean-washed beach,
where teenagers used to go surreptitiously to make out,
that's where he lay—
                blood from battle
still caked under his nails, his tight-chested
groans sounding above the trough
                        of quiet as the surf
collapsed, waves
                running in moonless darkness
up the shingle.
                His body on shore
and the vacuum opening up between him
and the stars—
                it must have made him

sicken to stare up into that space,
                              feel himself
whirling through such blackness—
as in a gas station
                    when you go to pay the attendant,
one of the service areas just off the Wilbur Cross or Merritt Parkway,
and you hear the cars' engine-surf
never ending as you step into the station,
shutting your eyes against the neon—
and darkness comes pouring out of some reservoir
inside you, thick and black as motor oil,
                              phosphenes
pricking your retinas so that your eyes
open into the eyes of the attendant,
                              holding his gaze
maybe a moment too long, trying to fight off
that giddy off-kilter whirling
of yourself still moving, the highway speeding
under you
            wanting to throw you off . . .
So it must have been for Achilles—
                              only,
much worse; feeling the waves' pounding
vibrate through the sand,
                    and the sand
always shifting above the earth turning
as he hunched on his side, then thrashed, turning
and turning on himself, burrowing like a wild creature
before contracting his huge body into a fetal position,
knees to chin, trying laboriously to sleep . . .

But when sleep finally took him, laving him,
soothing the pain afflicting heart and mind—
oh, how he ached, legs heavy as stone
from having run down Hector, sprinting round and round

wind-funneling Troy's walls—
                         there appeared
to him what looked like Patroclus,
wretched, dead Patroclus, the man's imago
framed as the very body of the dead one,
identical in voice and gaze, wearing Patroclus' clothes
as it kneeled down to his friend's ear and whispered:

"Achilles . . . how can you sleep?
When I was alive, you didn't neglect me.
But now, in death, you've forgotten me.
Bury me, Achilles—
                    the other dead, who
have stepped free of their bodies
and all their suffering, won't let me cross
the river to join them:
                        they drive me off, forcing
me to wander through Death's wide-gated house . . .
Reach out your hand to me: once you've burned
my body, I won't ever come to you again,
I'll never cross back through those wide gates . . .
It's hard to bear up under grief like this—
remember how we'd go off from all our other friends
and make our separate plans:
                            those times won't come again.
My fate, lying in wait for me from the moment
I was born, has devoured me in its jaws.
And your fate too, even though you're like a god,
is mine:
         to die under the high walls of Troy.

There's something more I want from you, Achilles:
once the fire eats into my bones, turning them
to ashes, I want your remains mixed with mine
in that urn of gold, the one with two handles

that your mother gave to you, your mother
like a queen —
                              but a queen who will never die."

Lightning-heeled Achilles answered:
"Patroclus, why did you come here to me — your face,
your head —
                    so dear, so familiar —
                                        to give me these commands?
I'll devote all my strength to fulfilling
everything you ask —
                              but come closer to me now —
I want to hold you, even if it's only for a little while,
lie down with me and join me in my grief."

Saying this, he reached out his arms,
reached them round
                              the other's shape,
but couldn't hold him:
                              the dream that was Patroclus
gave a faint cry
                    and sank like smoke into the earth.

Achilles' right hand gripped only
his left —
              he sat up, astonished —
                                        said, grieving:
"It's not his body, but the likeness of a man
that hovers in Death's house:
                              a shape of smoke
with no blood, no beating heart . . .
Poor Patroclus, shattered in his grief,
                                        his tears and moans
looking and sounding as real as mine —
                                        but it was only a shadow

that kneeled down beside me, telling me all its troubles
so that it seemed in every way like you,
Patroclus, all through the night kneeling here beside me."

So he spoke out his heart and aching mind:
the soldiers sleeping round him
                              heard him, woke—
and then gathered together, weeping,
as the dawn's
              flushed fingers stroked
the pale cheeks of Patroclus' corpse.

Airport Economy Inn

No one speaking, nothing moving

except for the way the snow keeps falling,
its falling a kind of talking in the dark
while all across the valley we keep on sleeping

in the separate conditions of our dreaming.

His face all overgrown with concern

the newsman's mouth says whatever it's saying,
explosions going off, sound turned down, wind
ripping at some twanging strip of metal.

My friend's voice keeps murmuring in my head,

murmuring she's stressed by going out

with two men at once, worrying they'll cross
and she'll lose them both, she's starting
to drink and smoke too much, love's

making her a liar, a chimney head, an alky.

No one speaking, nothing moving but snow

falling, falling, burying this motel
with its takeout menu, *New Standard Bible,*
checkout time 11 A.M.,

smiley face envelope to leave the maid a tip:

out in the hall someone's pounding

on the ice machine, one hand beating rhythm to
fuck it fuck it fuck it fuck it . . .
Reveries of living here year after year,

scalloped walls, cottage cheese ceiling,

plaster hands praying on the checkout counter,

complimentary donuts hoarded in the ice bucket
DO NOT DISTURB credit card imprint
Room 401's one of our regulars

. . . food, god, death, money, a TV clicker

to push the world back and bring it closer,

fantasies of lust so ridiculous and charmed
you need two king beds and a mirrored ceiling.
No one speaking, nothing moving

but for the screen lighting up with bombs falling

through shifting fortunes of the soldier

on a stretcher, body gone limp,
lost in glare spilling off a Humvee's side
that keeps hearse-like pace with the stretcher moving

above the stretcher's shadow.

No one speaking, nothing moving,

my eyes close, I drift and doze,
dissolving to jags, chunks, splinters,
flake piling on flake erasing diamond-cut angles

of every crystal swirling through streetlight

before fading back into parking lot gloom as these lines stretch out

and return to the margin
as if nothing can stop this pattern
from repeating, words

telling it in irregular shifts of rhythm

while the crawl keeps crawling at the bottom of the screen.

NOTES

"Blueprint": the ancient Greek word *menos* means something like "strength" or "life force," and *thumos* means "heart" or "center of motion and action."

"Oracle": "big boy" refers to early-model, liquid-propellant ICBMs—the Titan and the Atlas.

"Ice Trucker Pilgrimage: A Libretto": the last line is from the last diary entry of Robert Falcon Scott, the polar explorer.

"Drag Show": the last stanza is adapted from lines spoken by Lauren Bacall in *To Have and Have Not*.

"Persian Miniature": the quotation is from Sir Thomas Browne's *Religio Medici*.

"Zoom": *aere perennius* is a phrase from Horace (*Odes* 3.30) that translates "more lasting than bronze."

"The Flood": the quote is adapted from a statement by D. W. Winnicott.

"Airport Economy Inn": "the crawl" is network newspeak for the print news that streams across the bottom of the TV screen.